CHINGLISH

CHINGLISH
FOUND IN TRANSLATION

OLIVER
LUTZ
RADTKE

Gibbs Smith, Publisher
TO ENRICH AND INSPIRE HUMANKIND
Salt Lake City | Charleston | Santa Fe | Santa Barbara

First Edition
11 10 09   10 9 8 7

Text © 2007 Oliver Lutz Radtke

4

Published by
Gibbs Smith, Publisher
P.O. Box 667
Layton, Utah 84041

Orders: 1.800.835.4993
www.gibbs-smith.com

Designed by Raffi Ekmekjian, blackeye.com
Printed and bound in China

Library of Congress Cataloging-in-Publication Data
Library of Congress Control Number: 2007929321
ISBN 13 978-1-4236-0335-1
ISBN 10 1-4236-0335-4

RECOMMENDED READING

Engrish.com—the Japlish counterpart by Steve Caires

Hanzismatter.com—Chinese character tattoos go awry

Books

Melvyn Bragg, *The Adventure of English.*

David Crystal, *English as a Global Language.*

Joan Pinkham, *The Translator's Guide to Chinglish.*

Essays

Walter Benjamin, "The Task of the Translator," in *Illuminations: Essays and Reflections.*

Chen Meilin/Hu Xiaoqiong, "Towards the acceptability of China English."
http://journals.cambridge.org.

Liu et al., "Lost in Translation: Millions of Tourists to China are confused by a Myriad of 'Chinglish' Misinterpretations."
http://www.linguist.org.cn.

Niu Qiang/Martin Wolff, "China and Chinese, or Chingland and Chinglish?"
http://journals.cambridge.org.

Wei Yun/Fei Jia, "Using English in China. From Chinese Pidgin English through Chinglish to Chinese English and China English."
http://journals.cambridge.org.

S ome instances in life happen with such intensity that they may well be regarded as the starting point for a wonderful friendship or a lifelong passion. I had such a moment on July 25, 2000. I was about to get off a taxi near the Shanghai Foreign Languages University, where I had recently started my scholarship year as a Chinese major, when a neat sticker on the inside of the door told me: "Don't forget to carry your thing."

I was immediately fascinated, and I began to look everywhere for signs of "Chinglish." I traveled the provinces and spotted it throughout, often in the most unexpected places. I found it on hotel room doors and brightly lit highway billboards, construction sites and soccer balls, condoms and pencil boxes.

Chinglish exists because people travel and their language travels with them. Chinglish also exists because of China's opening to the world, the tourism industry, state propaganda mechanisms, and the Internet. In preparation for the 2008 Olympic Games, Beijing is gearing up an immense amount of manpower to eradicate Chinglish from the capital, and the Chinese government plans to extend this linguistic cleansing to the rest of the country as well. My aim is to show the nowadays endangered species of Chinglish in its natural habitat.

Many contributors to this book come from the academic world. Most of them fear their colleagues' reactions and are uncertain about having their names revealed. For my part, I am in the privileged position to stick my head out for something I regard well worth the risk—a better understanding between China and the world.

Since Chinese grammar is virtually nonexistent regarding inflections, declinations, and past and future tenses, it offers more options to play around than many other languages. This makes Chinese a first-class creativity booster. Linguistic variations exist in any language, including German, my mother tongue; these variations possess a creative potential that we should cherish more. The reinterpretation of language allows for a tremendous amount of humor, and humor is, and always has been, a cross-cultural form of communication. Therefore this book is about passion, not mockery. It is my most sincere hope that this book is understood as a bridge rather than a border.

Chinglish is very often funny because of the sometimes scarily direct nature of the new meaning produced by the translation. A "deformed man toilet" in Shanghai or an "anus hospital" in Beijing is funny because it instantly destroys linguistic euphemisms we Westerners have carefully built up when talking about sensitive topics. Chinglish annihilates these conventions right away. Chinglish is right in your face.

"Poetry is what gets lost in translation," writes American poet Robert Frost. In terms of Chinglish, he's plain wrong.

This book came as a surprise and the realization of a dream I have had for quite some time. Ever since I spotted my first Chinglish sign in Shanghai, I have wanted to let people know about this truly fascinating topic, and, more importantly, make them interested in China and its people.

I thank Gibbs Smith, Publisher for this opportunity, my editor Jared Smith for brushing up my Denglish, and especially Christopher Robbins for contacting me in the first place. Many thanks go to Nico Volland and Tia Thornton for their valuable comments and my friends and fellow travelers, especially Patricia Schetelig, who provided me with their Chinglish beauties over the years.

I thank my father for living the importance of writing every day.

And finally I'd like to thank you, dear reader, for picking up this little picture book and for your interest in a country that will continue to fascinate and divide for years to come.

Oliver Lutz Radtke

7

Nearly four hundred million people speak it as their mother tongue, another six hundred million as their second language. A billion are learning it, a third of the world's population is exposed to it, and *The Economist* predicts that by 2050 half the world will be in some way proficient in it: English is globalization's number one language, the communicative tool for trade, techniques, and tacticians in foreign ministries around the world. English, that local Germanic dialect spoken by one hundred fifty thousand people in the fifth century who survived the perpetual threat of extinction by Danish invaders, has come a long way indeed. Non-native speakers now outnumber native speakers by a ratio of about three to one. How likely (or desirable) is it that they all speak the same?

You might ask, what is Chinglish, anyway? It depends on whom you ask. Chinese emigrants raising their children in English-speaking countries will probably answer: Chinglish is a useful mix of Mandarin or Cantonese terms with day-to-day English. It is indeed convenient to shorten a sentence such as "I don't want to go now because it is too hot and it will be hard to find a parking lot anyway" into "Don't go la, hot la, tai mafan a." For the Chinese high-school teacher, Chinglish is the students' unsuccessful attempts to understand English through a Chinese matrix, resulting in sentences such as "Please hurry to walk or we'll be late" or "She was very miserable and her heart broke." However, the English-speaking traveler more frequently encounters Chinglish in the form of public signs rather than spoken oddities. This book displays examples of the latter category, since oral Chinglish is difficult to visualize. But no matter how one looks at the phenomenon, one thing is clear: Chinglish is not a language.

The harbinger of Chinglish might be found, according to some scholars, in Chinese Pidgin English, which came to life in the eighteenth century when the British established their first trading posts in Guangzhou. The term originated from the word "business" and served, according to the great Yale China scholar Jonathan Spence, "to keep the differing communities in touch, by mixing words from Portuguese, Indian, English, and various Chinese dialects, and spelling them according to Chinese syntax." Some believe that the idiomatic expressions "Long time no see" or "No can do" have originated from that time. Others refer to the late Qing-Dynasty Empress Dowager Cixi, who forced Chinese villagers to migrate to the West in the late nineteenth and early twentieth century. Another candidate is the so-called Yangjingbang 洋泾浜 (named after a long-gone creek in Shanghai near today's Yan'an Dong Lu, which had separated the British and French settlements), an integration of English into Mandarin in the era of Lu Xun, China's greatest twentieth-century writer. Very influential, too, are the large numbers of Chinese immigrants to the United States, not only those who came during the Gold Rush era but also those who, in the last twenty-five years since the beginning of China's policy of Reform and Opening, have emigrated in increasing numbers.

No matter which theory one prefers, two things are certain: first, Chinglish exists because people move, and second, as a linguistic phenomenon it is all but new. "The ignorance of English . . . sometimes leads to ludicrous mistakes, and we occasionally enjoy some very rich typographical errors in the Shanghai papers," wrote Carl Crow, one of China's best foreign chroniclers in the 1930s, in his memoir *400 Million Customers*. Crow, who ran Shanghai's first Western advertising agency, fumed over the sloppiness with which printers added at goodwill translations of their texts in foreign letters, since "the text means little more to them than the text of a Chinese advertisement means to the foreign auditor." Errors keep coming all the more in our time, largely thanks to the Internet.

Many problems arise not from spelling mistakes but from a poor understanding of the cultural context into which one must translate. Language always embodies cultural context and a translator, ideally, is capable of translating into that different cultural setting. "To cast pearls before swine" is in Chinese "playing the cittern for an ox" or dui niu tan qin 对牛弹琴. For hu tou she wei 虎头蛇尾 ("tigerhead and snaketail") Shakespeare is simply perfect: much ado about nothing. But also sometimes a bookworm is just a "bookworm": shuchong 书虫. English may be defined as a hypotactic language whereas Chinese is rather paratactic. English relies heavily on a logical sequence; Chinese is deeply rooted in its graphic imagery. Both have their advantages. And both need to be taken into consideration when attempting to cross the cultural border. That is why a word-by-word translation usually fails or produces unintelligible content which is at best humorous if not hazardous at times. "Be careful to fall in the water" is a perfect one-to-one translation of xiaoxin diaoxia shui 小心掉下水 that just follows the Chinese syntax. According to Joan Pinkham and her unique read *The Translator's Guide to Chinglish,* unnecessary words are the trademark of Chinglish translations: "these constitute important conditions in striving for the fulfilment of the general task in the transitional period" clearly needs some polishing. Another classic example is the tendency toward nominal style, such as, "The prolongation of the existence of their temple is due to the solidity of its construction." Another common problem is wrong word order—"I tomorrow will go to Shanghai"—as directly translated from Chinese or outdated words.

With so many snake pits around the task of translation, you probably end up with the most-asked question: "Why is nobody checking?" I've invested a great deal of time, money, and beer bills in trying to figure out what the thought processes of sign makers in China are—a question, I believe, that touches on general concepts that China and her citizens have about themselves and the world. I think it is valid to ask why nobody actually proofreads many of the bilingual signs in China—signs that are not only displayed publicly but brightly illuminated by night, enlarged to giant proportions as billboard ads or larger-than-life posters. Possible approaches to China's bilingual sign makers are:

1. Nobody speaks English in China
I think we can dismiss this notion right away. There are not only enough foreigners in China

who could do the job, but—more importantly—enough Chinese university graduates with excellent language skills, even more so when they return from abroad. Having said that, I have to add that young Chinese who speak and write fluent English usually don't work as translators, which is considered by many as a side job. Most English native speakers, on the other hand, lack sufficient command of Chinese that would allow them to take the job. That many Chinese students struggle with the English language, hence the abundant Chinese academic literature on classroom Chinglish, is well-known, but not relevant here.

2. We don't care
No matter if it is right or wrong, as long as it looks foreign, cool, and different, we are fine with it. This approach highly appeals to me not only because of garbled English phrases but also because of the countless unintelligible Hanyu pinyin signs—gibberish pinyin if you like—where it is highly unclear to me who the target group for this line of nonsense Latin characters is. PR progression made in China might be: A sign in Chinese is standard, a sign in Chinese and gibberish pinyin is better, and a sign in Chinese and something resembling English is best of all. This, of course, isn't called translating, but decorating. English words are placed solely for domestic consumers. They are meant for display, not for information. That helps to explain why one finds "Are you praised when it's great?" on men's underwear in China.

3. We don't know any better
Those familiar with certain company structures in China know to what I am referring. Dongfeng Gongsi needs a new company sign that is bilingual and international looking. Who is taking charge of that? Little Wang, of course! Why? 因为他英文是最好的 Because his English is the best! But what does that really mean? Poor Little

Wang has to deal with something he might not be familiar with at all, but his superiors regard his English to be the best—in the company. So naturally he gets selected for the task. No one notices the problems afterwards because his boss's English is virtually nonexistent, so nobody bothers.

4. We want to do it ourselves
This would be a discussion about "losing face": how come we've built the Great Wall and the Forbidden City and now need to rely on red-haired barbarians helping us with their language! An unlikely but possible scenario.

5. The might of online translation tools
It is quite likely that many sign manufacturers (and poor Little Wang) are actually relying on free online software to generate their characteristic word-by-word translations. To test this theory I selected two of my collection's catchier phrases and ran translation quests on five different Web sites:

先下后上，文明乘车 (After first under on, do riding with civility)
(1) After first under on, the civilization rides in a carriage
(2) Go down upper, civilized riding of queen first
(3) After descending first up, the civilization goes by car
(4) After the jump, civilized ride
(5) Under on, the civilization rides in a carriage after first

残疾人厕所 (Deformed man toilet)
(1) Disabled person restroom
(2) Deformed man toilet (!)
(3) Disable and sick person's toilet

(4) Disabled toilet
(5) Disabled person restroom

Obviously, better translators are needed. But what does that mean? I believe that a translator doesn't only feature bilingual skills but also embodies a bicultural vision. She has to successfully mediate between cultures, including different political systems and moral and social structures, to really overcome the incompatibilities that stand in her way to a successful transfer of meaning. Translators have to be aware of their unique position, that of a privileged reader whose job extends far beyond finding the right words, to include finding the right color, taste, and sound in a completely different setting. In his essay "The Task of the Translator," German philosopher Walter Benjamin demands that "[a] real translation is transparent; it does not cover the original, does not block its light, but allows the pure language, as though reinforced by its own medium, to shine upon the original all the more fully." He demands a lot there, but a lot might improve already when this is only partially taken into account. I also recommend thinking about the following basic aspects:

周 Better dictionaries
Languages live; they evolve and change, constantly. Although it is a costly process, dictionaries, nevertheless, have to try to keep up with that.

周 Better feel of the audience
For whom are you actually translating? Is this sign really seen by foreigners?

周 Better attitude
China joined the World Trade Organization in 2001. If companies want to compete globally and signs are not just supposed to be cool, they have to play by the rules.

周 Better not translate everything

Chinese fermented soy milk is of course bean curd but dofu sounds much tastier and we are accustomed to it. This piece of advice, of course, demands lots of time, until citizens in Western countries won't order their Chinese food by numbers but instead by accurately using a dish's real name. I am sure, though, that day will come.

"East is East and West is West and never the twain shall meet," said Rudyard Kipling. He is wrong, too. With Chinglish they do. And they will continue to do so since Beijing is fighting an uphill battle with its cleansing campaigns. I fully understand the Chinese government's attempt to eradicate false signs that could lead to potentially dangerous situations: an allergic person that doesn't recognize certain ingredients in a potentially hazardous dish, a swimmer who isn't warned about the dangerous waters ahead of him, and so on. But most Chinglish isn't solely incorrect, it is creative and—what is more—the "twisted" use of English in China presents a window through which the open-minded visitor can establish a preliminary feeling as to how the Chinese think and how their language embodies their own culture.

Besides: Chinglish just won't die. The Global Language Monitor reports that 20 percent of the twenty thousand new English words and phrases it recorded in 2005 were Chinglish, including "drinktea," meaning "closed," and its opposite, "torunbusiness," meaning "open." You may have already used "the Gang of Four" or "pay New Year calls" and "give face." I truly believe that there are an endless amount of mistakes made by English (and German) native speakers in Chinese. Bad Chinese by foreigners is rarely documented on signs and gateways, leaving virtually no publishable examples. But I'd be happy to cooperate on that equally fascinating topic.

To translate appropriately is a high form of art that is not grasped by simply knowing a language. A high-class translation comes about only through a detailed understanding of cultural backgrounds and great sensitivity to miniscule language differences.

The author of this book is a young, partially China-trained, German sinologist. He has a wakeful eye for all things Chinese and a solid understanding of why the Chinese, under the influence of their country's opening to the world, take so much interest in studying foreign languages. It is because of his exploring spirit that you now hold this book in your hands.

Language and thinking are closely intertwined. This book provides the reader the opportunity to explore the Chinese mind, their language and creativity. It serves as an interesting and insightful guide not only for translators, students, and teachers of Chinese but also for anyone involved in the discovery of a foreign language.

Susian Stähle
Chinese lecturer
Heidelberg University
Institute for Chinese Studies

Roast duck of Beijing
Rinse the meat of Beijing
Wheat Joss-stick Cow Willow
Fried peanut
Korea Form Dog meat
The temple explodes the chicken cube
The meat mixs the bean curd
Fragrant and hot soil bean silk
The meat fries the mushroom
mountain wild vegetable
the beer braises the persimmon
The dry fried Huang's flower fish
Dumpling
Fried rice
Fried noodle

Welcome the foreign friend come

请照看好您的小孩,不要在店堂内奔跑、打闹
No romping in the hall

先下后上　文明乘车

After first under on, do riding with civility.

上海地铁运营有限公司　服务监
Shanghai Metro Operation Co.,LTD

2	伏特加	Vodka	50.00
2	白兰地	Cognac	55.00
2	威士忌	Whisky	50.00
2	啤酒	Beer	10.00
2	矿泉水	Water	10.00
2	可口可乐	Coca Cola	10.00
2	雪碧	Sprite	10.00
2	纯牛奶	Pure Milk	10.00
2	杏仁露	Almond juice	10.00
2	方便面	Advantageous noodle	10.00
6	干果	Cashews pistachios	30.00
2	巧克力	Chocolate	20.00
3	润喉糖	Gum	25.00
总数 Total			

房号:

日期:

Date

24

取 水 处
TAKEWATERPLACE

注意防滑
ADVERT SKIDPROOF

东 湖 之 旅

洗
发
液
Sham Poo

老人、儿童上扶梯时
需有家人陪同

When old man's child go up hand ladder
temporary need the family to accompany

32

如遇紧急情况请速拨打：

Meeting critical situation asks velocity to poke strikeing :

报警电话：2431027 内线：6114

Alarm reporting telephone : 2431027 Sec et agent: 6114

骑驴上坡骑驴下　没啦坐个好车马

如今交通大变化　出门打的坐小巴

The horse carriage used in ancient time is equivalent to Mercedes Benz today, it ranks very high.

严禁吸烟

NO SMOKING

—— 一根火柴可以毁掉百年宫殿

A SMALL MATCH MAY DISTROY
A HUNDRED YEAR-OLD PALACE.

Dried turnip and

8元/份

夫妻肺片

Man and wife lung slice

18元/份

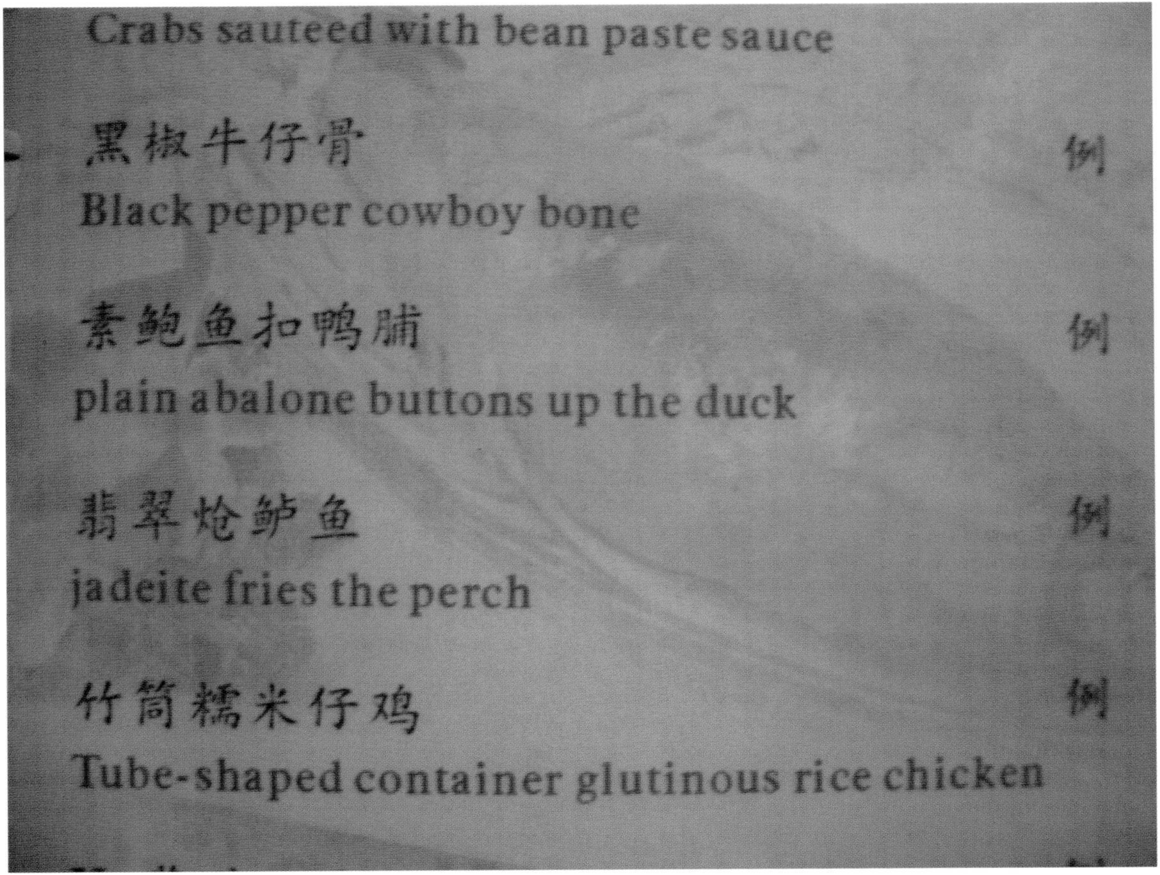

Crabs sauteed with bean paste sauce

黑椒牛仔骨

例

Black pepper cowboy bone

素鲍鱼扣鸭脯

例

plain abalone buttons up the duck

翡翠炝鲈鱼

例

jadeite fries the perch

竹筒糯米仔鸡

例

Tube-shaped container glutinous rice chicken

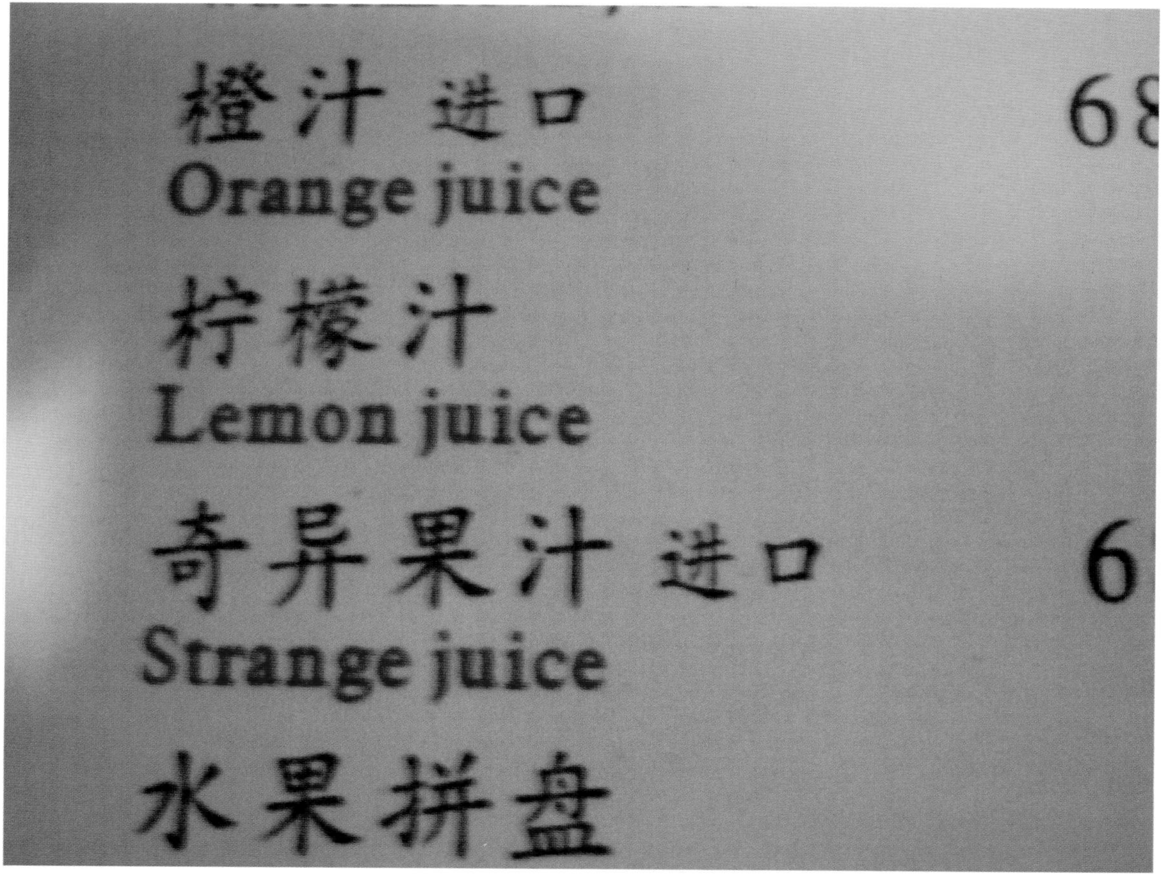

橙汁 进口　68

Orange juice

柠檬汁

Lemon juice

奇异果汁 进口　6

Strange juice

水果拼盘

向自觉维护公共
卫生的游客致敬

**SALUTE TO THE TOURISTS WHO
KEEP THE PUBLIC HYGIENCE**

42

游人止步

The visitor halts

44

Le Quai
奇楼阁
RESTAURANT & LOUNGE

☐ Baby Vegetble with Anchovy dressry   RMB 35. × ☐
马赛港银鱼酱嫩时蔬

☐ Roasted Prawns with Herbs   RMB 50. × ☐
香烤凤尾虾

☐ Deep-fried Seasame Children Stick   RMB 50. × ☐
with Tartar Sauce
撒旦脆皮芝麻鸡条

☐ Sicily Assorted Garlic bread (4Pcs)   RMB 35. × ☐
西西里什锦蒜茸面包

☐ Special B.B.Q Pork Pastry   RMB 35. × ☐
秘制叉烧酥

☐ Golden Braised Pork with Rice   RMB 35. × ☐
金牌卤肉饭

☐ Spice Beef Tenden   RMB 50. × ☐
麻辣牛筋

☐ Crisp Fish & Almond   RMB 50. × ☐
丁香杏仁

Total（总计）: RMB _____

This B action movie is shot with a bit more competence than other films in the ge
It also looks like it had a generous budget, or at least a lot of cooperation from t
Philippine army, judging by the amount of gunfights, soldiers, Armored Personnel
Carriers and explosions that feature throughout the film. The plot is the old "rescue
my 'Nam buddy from the rank jungle prison he's being held in by the psychotic
Communist general with thousands of troops under his command" premise. The good
guys are invincible, the bad guys thoroughly expendable. You know what to expect.
Sit back and let our boys win one for the Gipper. I must add in closing that Thomaslan
Griffith really is a good actor- I hope he gets cast in more mainstream films in the
future.

特別部隊成員米奇與拍檔鍾
斯在中越邊境，搶走越南將軍的
核子引爆器；一輪混戰中，鍾斯
被越南人捉走，米奇僥倖逃脫，
但情急之下將引爆器收藏。一年
後，米奇喬裝遊客重臨越南，卻
被越南將軍捉拿，逼他說出引爆
器下落。米奇與鍾斯的生命繫於

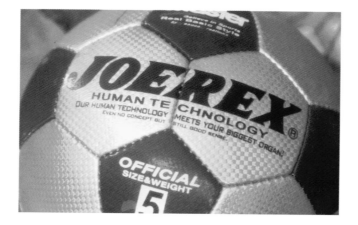

办公室

The thing tube office

FOREVER MEMORY

Even goldfish need love.......
especially on rainy days.

THE LAST SAMURAI

最后武士

"A gorgeously filmed study of homosexuallust."

Melanie McFarland, SEATTLE TIMES

接送站
停车位
THE PLACE OF
RECEIVEOR
泰安交通局监制

不可回收
UNRECYCLE RUBDISH

依依芳草 敬请爱怜
SHOW MERCY
TO THE SLENDER GRASS

当心滑跌

TAKE CARE OF YOUR SLIP

FATTY CAT PIPI
PIPI IS A VERY CUTE FATTY CAT

☒ The Pipi cat likes to eat
Doughnut.
Its name is Pipi, a very fatty cat.
Its favorite foods are fish, cake,
sandwich.
The sports it likes most is to
bite the navel, to bath.
It is a very naughty cat.

© CHYUAN SHYANG STATIONERY CO. PD 015

S-3980

ABC

Operating hours: 1: 30 pm to 10:00 pm
Tel.Ext.: 63819

KTV 包房

美国 BOSE 音响，幽雅、浪漫，给您全新的感受。

位置：　　　　　酒店三层
营业时间：　　14：00 至次日凌晨 1：00
电话分机：　　63812

KTV PRIVATE ROOM

American BOSE sound equipment sets the tone for an entire new feeling here: exquisite, romantic, can't you touch it?

Location: the 3rd floor
Operating hours: 2: 00 pm to 1:00 an next day
Tel.Ext.: 63812

台球、棋牌

斯诺克台球、棋类、麻将等多种娱乐用具，总有一款适合您。

位置：　　　　　酒店四层
营业时间：　　13：30 至 24：00

Location: the 4th Floor
Operating hours: 2：00 pm to 2:00 am next day
Tel.Ext.:   63813

燕山酒城 因装修暂停营业
温馨典雅，酒浓情浓，尽享浪漫情怀。
位置：   酒店三层
营业时间：   19：00 至次日凌晨 1：00
电话分机：   63811

YOUNGSUN BAR Temporarily closed for inside decoration
The intoxicating beverage will lead you into an intoxicating cosmos, please soak up the romantic atmosphere.
Location: the 3rd Floor
Operating hours: 7:00 pm to 1:00 am next day
Tel.Ext.:   63811

本大廳已全面消毒，
請安心使用。
The store be sterilized inside ,
please be contented .

九三年 **04** 月 **23** 日

關西服務區　新東陽　HSIN TUNG YANG　關心您

人与花木 呼吸互动 摘花折木 自减生命

People, flowers and help each other in breath.If you pluck the flowers and break off the branches, you will reduce your own life at the same time.

← 距长城760m
The Great Wall

請妥善保管您的明細表

請勿隨手棄置

以免歹徒竊取您的帳戶資料

PLEASE DON'T DUMP YOUR RECEIPT
AND KEEP IT CAREFULLY TO AVOID
GANGSTER GET YOUR INFORMATION

台新銀行

表出口

佛教圣地，清净庄严，
洗心池内，严禁乱丢。

Washing　heart pool, So pure and so clean,
Holy buddhism land, No Litter into please.

南普陀寺日

为了您的安全，老人、儿童、病人需有人陪同登阁参观。

Take good care of the old man children and Patient

You provide my best friend
You provide me with joy and love...

The past is like a dream brimful of sweet memories, warm feelings and loving thoughts. Cranes have grown and climbed all over my wall of yearning.

FOR MY SPECIAL FRIEND

康乐设施
HEALTH & FITNESS FACILITIES

保龄球

期望您在潇洒的击打中，感受成功的快乐。

位置：　　　　　　酒店四层
营业时间：　　　　13：30---24：00
电话分机：　　　　63818

BOWLING

The splendid joy of success is waving to you in your wonderful bowling.

Location:　　　　the 4th Floor
Operating hours:　1：30 p m to 0:00 am next day
Tel.Ext.:　　　　63818

健身房

齐全的器械，优美的场地，将使您轻松愉悦、身心俱佳。

A thing all to see is of value
Well! let's go out to the town

PERSON SPORTS

It helps! Are you praised
when it is great?

惠多　　　门垫

美化空间　　美化生活

Bath&kitchen　　Mat

This comfortably makes me feel so good.

無ㄨ障ㄓㄤ礙ㄞˋ坡ㄆㄛ道ㄉㄠ
Disability-Free Slope

徐家汇派出所

警方提示
Police tips

千日防贼，
Avoiding being stolen should

不可一日松懈；
be always remembered.

居安思危，
Be prepared for danger in

务须警钟长鸣。
times of safety.

徐家汇派出所宣

BIG
DOGGIE

LUSTFUL PIG

I'M A LUSTFUL AND BAD PIG.
DOGLIKE FIGURE IS MY CHARACTER AND FRIENDS
CALLED ME "DOGGIE" MY BEST HOBBY
IS TO COLLECT COLOR PANTIES.
LUSTFULPIG-DOGGIE.

★★★★ IT IS FINE TODAY! LUSTFUL PIG DOGGIE ★★★★

存取款一体机
Cash Recycling Machine

THIS RARE **NOTE BOOK** IS JUST FOR YOU

Our finest quality paper
ensures a smooth surface that
is a pleasure to write on.
This is the most comfortable
notebook you have ever run into.
You will feel like writing
with it all the time.

YOU & I

I have the heart for you, to build the tower of love.

生离死别最心伤　儿女送葬哭爹娘

年年上坟烧柱香　世俗人情万年长

Holding funeral rite is an old
custom when the people dead.
Today, most people enjoy modern
custom.

請勿忘隨身物品

DON'T FORGET TO CARRY YOUR THING

PHOTO CREDITS